T0040692

A Pack of
Wolves
and Other Canine Groups

Anna Claybourne

Heinemann
LIBRARY
Chicago, Illinois

H **www.capstonepub.com**
Visit our website to find out more information about Heinemann-Raintree books.

To order:
☎ Phone 800-747-4992
💻 Visit www.capstonepub.com
to browse our catalog and order online.

© 2013 Heinemann Library
an imprint of Capstone Global Library, LLC
Chicago, Illinois

All rights reserved. No part of this publication may be reproduced or transmitted in any form or by any means, electronic or mechanical, including photocopying, recording, taping, or any information storage and retrieval system, without permission in writing from the publisher.

Edited by Nancy Dickmann, Adam Miller, and Laura Knowles
Designed by Richard Parker
Original illustrations © Capstone Global Library Ltd 2013
Illustrations by Jeff Edwards
Picture research by Ruth Blair

Originated by Capstone Global Library Ltd

Library of Congress Cataloging-in-Publication Data
Claybourne, Anna.
  A pack of wolves, and other canine groups / Anna Claybourne.
      p. cm.—(Animals in groups)
  Includes bibliographical references and index.
  ISBN 978-1-4329-6482-5 (hb)—ISBN 978-1-4329-6489-4 (pb) 1. Gray wolf—Juvenile literature. 2. Canidae—Juvenile literature. I. Title.
  QL737.C22C59 2013
  599.773—dc23   2011038138

Acknowledgments
We would like to thank the following for permission to reproduce photographs: Alamy: Arco Images GmbH, 14; Getty Images: Michael Sewell, 19, S.J. Krasemann, 34, Steve Kaufman, 18; iStockphoto: Andy Gehrig, 28, Keith Szafranski, 17, Nathan Hobbs, 41; Nature Picture Library: ARCO, 23, Edwin Giesbers, 15, Eric Baccega, 7, 13, Jeff Vanuga, 40, Laurent Geslin, 27, Mark Carwardine, 33, Nick Garbutt, 37, Philippe Clement, 35, Staffan Widstrand, 24, Steven Kazlowski, 9, Suzi Eszterhas, 39; Shutterstock: Biskariot, 32, Chris Alcock, Cover, Francois van Heerden, 38, Geoffrey Kuchera, 20, Kane513, 11, Lori Labrecque, 8, Maxim Kulko, 31, Ronnie Howard, 5, Torsten Lorenz, 29, Wild At Art, 4

Every effort has been made to contact copyright holders of any material reproduced in this book. Any omissions will be rectified in subsequent printings if notice is given to the publisher.

Disclaimer
All the Internet addresses (URLs) given in this book were valid at the time of going to press. However, due to the dynamic nature of the Internet, some addresses may have changed, or sites may have changed or ceased to exist since publication. While the author and publisher regret any inconvenience this may cause readers, no responsibility for any such changes can be accepted by either the author or the publisher.

Contents

DID YOU KNOW?

Discover amazing facts about wolves.

HUMAN INTERACTION

Find out what happens when humans and wolves come into contact with each other.

Some words are shown in bold, **like this**. You can find out what they mean by looking in the glossary.

HABITAT IN DANGER

Learn how wolves' habitats are under threat, and what is being done to protect them.

Welcome to the Pack!

When you think of a wolf, you might think of wolves in movies, cartoons, and fairy tales. Some are shown as wild, bloodthirsty beasts, howling at the Moon. They also appear as werewolves (half wolf and half human creatures) in horror stories, or as the big, bad villain who eats Red Riding Hood's grandmother.

The members of a wolf pack are loyal to each other.

DID YOU KNOW?

The gray wolf has the Latin scientific name *Canis lupus*. Each subspecies has a third part to its name. For example, the Arctic wolf is *Canis lupus arctos*.

Wolves in the wild

So, what are real wolves like? You might be surprised. Although they can be fierce, they are shy, clever animals. They rarely attack humans. They like being with other wolves and live in a close family group, or pack. They hunt together, share food, and defend each other from danger. They snuggle up together and nuzzle and lick each other. They have amazing ways of communicating, too.

Most wild wolves belong to just one **species**, the gray wolf. However, there are many types, or **subspecies**, of gray wolf. They can be dark or light gray, white, black, brown, or reddish in color.

Wolves really do howl. This gray wolf is probably calling to other pack members.

HUMAN INTERACTION

The domestic dog, the type people keep as pets, is actually thought to be a type of gray wolf. Over time, humans have tamed them and created different dog breeds. But they are still all the same species.

Who Lives in a Wolf Pack?

A gray wolf pack is almost always a family group—just like a human family. There are usually between 4 and 12 wolves in a pack, although scientists have discovered some packs with more than 30 members.

The leaders of the pack are the mother and father wolves, sometimes called the **breeding pair**. They are also sometimes known as the **alpha** female and alpha male. Every year, they have a **litter** of cubs, adding to the pack. The older cubs help to care for the babies. Sometimes other wolves who are not family members are in the pack, too.

Here you can see how the wolves in a pack of 11 could be related:

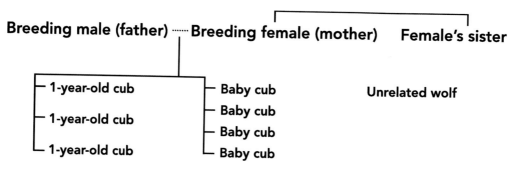

Breeding male (father) ······ Breeding female (mother)		Female's sister
1-year-old cub	Baby cub	Unrelated wolf
1-year-old cub	Baby cub	
1-year-old cub	Baby cub	
	Baby cub	

Why live in a pack?

Because wolves are social animals, they like being together. Living in a pack also helps them survive. By sharing food and tasks such as hunting, they can stay safer. For example, one wolf can take the job of guarding the cubs, while others go hunting. Then the hunters bring back food for the cubs and the babysitter.

DID YOU KNOW?

When a male and female wolf get together to start a pack and have cubs, they stay together as a couple for their whole lives.

The members of this Eurasian wolf pack are on the alert. They may have spotted **prey** or wolves from another pack.

We're in charge!

The breeding male and female lead the pack together. They make decisions such as when to go hunting or where to make a **den**. They also teach their cubs how to **track**, hunt, and fight.

The other wolves in the pack, including the cubs and the other adults, are known as **subdominant**. This means they respect the leaders and let them take control. Wolves have ways of showing each other their position in the pack. For example, a subdominant wolf may roll on its back and show its stomach to its leader (see page 21).

This is a breeding pair of timber wolves.

HUMAN INTERACTION

Scientists once thought that wolves in a pack would fight each other for power. Now, however, they think this does not happen much in the wild. It only happens when wolves are kept in **captivity**—for example, in a zoo. In a situation like this, a wolf cannot leave the pack easily, and so fights can break out.

On the sidelines

If the pack has extra wolves that are not part of the main family, they are subdominant. They have to know their place and never try to take power from the leading pair. If each wolf sticks to its role, the pack can stay together without trouble.

Sometimes a wolf does live by itself, as a "lone wolf." It may be a young wolf looking for a **mate** or an older wolf that has become separated from its pack.

Scientists sometimes capture a wild wolf to fit a radio collar on to it, so they can track its movements.

A place to live

Although a wolf pack itself may be small, it has a large **territory**. This is an area of land that the pack guards and patrols. The pack will travel around its territory most of the time, following prey animals and hunting them. It also defends its territory fiercely against other wolf packs.

A typical wolf territory will cover roughly 77 square miles (200 square kilometers), which is about the size of a large city. In some areas, where there is not much prey, territories can be as big as 1,160 square miles (3,000 square kilometers).

Keep off our patch!

Wolves constantly mark their territory as a signal to other wolf packs. They leave scent markers such as urine (liquid waste) and droppings (solid waste) around the territory. They also make scratch marks on the ground and howl to let other wolves know they are there.

If wolves do invade each other's territory, things can get nasty. A pack will fight viciously to keep out unknown wolves, and often these fights end in death. Therefore, wolves will usually avoid the edges of their territory, where they might bump into neighbors. However, if they meet a very young and helpless wolf from another pack, they may accept it into their pack instead.

HABITAT IN DANGER

A wolf pack needs a big territory to be able to find enough prey. Humans sometimes endanger wolves by taking over **wilderness** for farmland or housing, destroying the wolves' wild **habitat**.

Two wolves bare their teeth and stare hard at each other, to show they are ready to fight.

How Do Wolves Have Babies?

In a wolf pack, the only wolves that have babies are the breeding pair—the pack leaders. They have a litter of cubs every year, usually in the spring. The female makes a den to have her babies in. It can be a hole dug in the ground, a cave or hollow, or a sheltered spot between rocks or trees. There are between two and twelve cubs in a litter, but usually about six.

What are wolf cubs like?

Baby wolves are known as cubs or pups. When they are born, they are tiny. They weigh only about a hundredth of the weight of an adult wolf. Their eyes are closed and they cannot see or hear. But they already have a fluffy, furry coat. Once they are a few weeks old, wolf cubs love to play. They jump and skip, roll downhill, and chase and play-fight each other.

Like all **mammal** babies, the cubs feed on their mother's milk at first. Then, after a few weeks, their mother and the other wolves in the pack **regurgitate** food for them. This means they bring up food they have already swallowed and feed it to the cubs from their mouths.

DID YOU KNOW?

When wolf cubs are born, their eyes are bright blue. They gradually change to a yellowish-green color by the age of about four months.

Here, an Arctic wolf cub emerges watchfully from the safety of its den.

A pack of parents

As the cubs get older, the wolves in the pack all help to take care of them. The bigger wolves bring back meat for the babies and guard them from danger. They also teach the cubs to fight and hunt.

This older wolf is sharing a piece of meat with two of the pack's cubs.

HUMAN INTERACTION

There are many stories and reports of wolves caring for human children as their own. One example is the tale of Elmira Godayatova from Azerbaijan, in eastern Europe. She went missing in 1970, at age six, in the forest near her home. She was found safe and well 23 days later, saying she had been cared for by wolves.

Growing up

As they grow, wolf cubs go through a lot of changes:

10–12 days:	Eyes open
2–3 weeks:	Start growing teeth
3 weeks:	Start hearing
4–5 weeks:	Start eating regurgitated meat
6–8 weeks:	Start leaving the den
10–12 weeks:	Follow the other wolves on hunting trips
5–6 months:	Start joining in with hunts
8 months:	Reach adult size

When the cubs are a year old, their parents will probably have a new litter. For a while, the older cubs stay to care for the babies and to hunt for food to share. But when they are two or three years old, young wolves are often ready to have their own cubs. They usually leave the pack to find their own mates and start new packs somewhere else. Sometimes, though, they stay as pack members.

Cubs play-fight as a way to learn fighting and hunting methods—and to have fun together.

How Do Wolves Communicate?

To survive, wolves need to be able to "talk" to each other about many things, such as who's who in the pack, when to begin a hunt, or when danger is near.

Making a noise

Wolves can bark loudly or make a "whuffing" sound to alert other wolves to danger. Growling is used as a threat or warning, to show another wolf who is boss. Whimpering is the opposite. It means "we're friends" or "take care of me." There is also rallying, which is a mixture of wailing and yapping. Wolves use it to gather the pack together and show they are willing to do as they are told.

Why do wolves howl?

Wolves are famous for their long, high-pitched howls. They howl to tell each other where they are, to call the pack when they find food, and to get the pack together for a journey or a hunt. They may also howl when one member of the pack has died.

When a pack of wolves howl together, it sounds as if there are a lot of them, even if there are only a few. This is a useful way to warn other wolf packs off their territory. Other wolves will hear the sound of a big wolf pack, so they are more likely to stay away.

Did you know?

Wolves do not howl at the Moon, but they do howl more on lighter nights. This could simply be because lighter nights are better for hunting.

A wolf can hear another wolf's howl up to 9 miles (15 kilometers) away.

Sniffing power

Wolves are very good at smelling. Their sense of smell is around 100 times better than a human's, and it is an important way to communicate.

A wolf knows if another wolf is a friend or a stranger just from the smell it leaves behind. The smell of a wolf's urine can also tell other wolves if it is male or female, a breeding pack leader, or a subdominant wolf.

Wolves sniff to check which other wolves have passed the same way.

HABITAT IN DANGER

Wolves use scent markings to mark out a large territory. If humans take over wild land and use it for farming, building, or roads, it can break up the wolves' habitat. This can make it harder for the wolves to patrol and mark their territory.

Scent glands

Wolves have special scent **glands** on their faces, between their toes, and around their tails. As they run, sniff at things, and nuzzle other wolves, they leave scent markings using these glands. They can mark territory or make a scent trail for other pack members to follow.

When a pack of wolves are together, they will rub and nuzzle against each other. This helps to pass the pack scent around, so that all the wolves have the same smell. Pack members sniff and nuzzle new cubs, too. They learn the smell of the cubs and also mark them with the pack scent.

A gray wolf in Montana marks the winter snow with scent, using its feet.

Body language

Many animals use body language, including humans. You can often tell if a person is bored, excited, or unfriendly from his or her body position or movements. A tiger's flattened ears show it is angry, and a snake rears up when it is about to strike. For wolves, body language is even more important. They use the way they stand or sit and their ears, tails, and teeth to "talk" to other wolves.

The wolf that is lying down is using his body language to show he is less dominant than the other.

DID YOU KNOW?

Wolves make their fur bristle and stand on end when they are fighting or in danger. It makes their body look bigger and stronger, to scare their enemies.

What do they mean?

A wolf uses its body positions to show other wolves its place in the pack, its mood, or what it wants to do. Here are some of them:

I'm in charge.

I'm a subordinate— you're in charge!

I'm backing down.

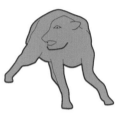
I'm ready to fight.

I want to play!

I'm scared!

I'm on the lookout.

HUMAN INTERACTION

Since pet dogs are closely related to wild wolves, they have many of the same body postures. This means human dog-owners can sometimes use body language to understand and communicate with their dog. For example, a dog stares without blinking when it is angry, but it blinks when it is being friendly.

What Do Wolves Eat?

Wolves are carnivores, or meat-eaters. They usually get their food by hunting, catching, and killing prey. Working together, they can bring down large grazing animals such as deer, musk oxen, or moose. They will also hunt smaller prey such as rabbits, mice, and fish.

Dead meat

If they cannot find fresh food, wolves will eat . This means the bodies of animals that are already dead and starting to rot. That might sound disgusting, but lots of wild animals do this. It is a way to use up food that would otherwise be wasted.

Wolves also create carrion for other species. When they have finished eating, then other animals, such as bears and vultures, come and eat the leftover scraps of meat and bone. Carrion-eating birds called ravens have even been seen hanging around animals that wolves like to prey on. The ravens call loudly, and the wolves follow them to find the prey. Then, once the wolves have fed, the ravens get their reward!

Meat-free meals

Wolves prefer meat, but if they are hungry, they will eat berries, plant buds, or other animals' eggs. If they live near human homes, they sometimes search through garbage cans.

HUMAN INTERACTION

Throughout history, farmers have hated wolves because they steal their animals. To protect their animals, farmers have often killed wolves by shooting or poisoning them. This is partly why some types of wolves are now **endangered**.

A large deer makes a fresh meal for this hungry wolf pack.

Meals on the move

Wolves like to hunt grass-eating animals such as wild sheep and reindeer, which tend to wander around a lot. So the wolves have to follow them, and they can travel up to 60 miles (100 kilometers) in one day.

A wolf's body is well **adapted** for covering long distances. Its long legs mean it has a large stride and can move fast without using up much energy. In northern, snowy parts of the world, wolves have large feet with slightly webbed toes. This helps them walk and run over snow without sinking in. Wolves also have great stamina, which means they can keep going all day without getting exhausted.

A Eurasian gray wolf pack makes its way across the snow in Russia.

DID YOU KNOW?

For long-distance travel, wolves trot at 5 to 6 miles (8 to 10 kilometers) per hour. But to catch prey, they can run at a top speed of about 37 miles (60 kilometers) per hour.

Wolves and the food web

Wolves play an important part in the **ecosystem**, which is their habitat and the creatures that live in it. By eating plant-eaters, they control their numbers. This allows plants to grow more and provide a home for insects and birds. Many animals also depend on leftovers from wolf kills.

However, wolves do not usually get eaten themselves, because they are at the top of the **food chain**. Their main enemies are humans who want to get rid of them to protect farm animals.

In this diagram of a **food web** in a northern pine forest, arrows point from each living thing to an animal that eats it.

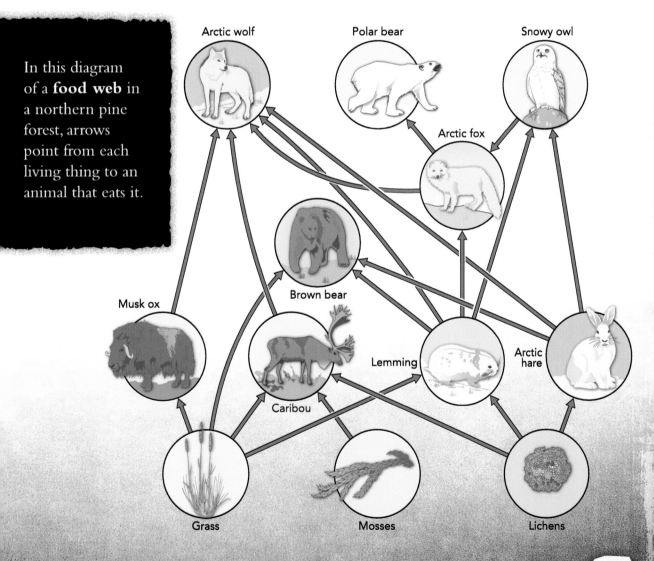

Arctic wolf

Polar bear

Snowy owl

Arctic fox

Brown bear

Musk ox

Lemming

Arctic hare

Caribou

Grass

Mosses

Lichens

Finding prey

Wolves track down their prey using smell and sight. Once they find something tasty, such as a herd of deer, they will follow the herd to tire the animals out. They might also charge at them, making them scatter, to find out which animals are weak or injured. These make the best targets, as they are easier to catch.

DID YOU KNOW?

Working together, a wolf pack can catch and kill an animal such as an elk or musk ox. These animals might be 10 times bigger and heavier than a single wolf.

Closing in

Next, the wolf pack splits up to surround one animal. They force it away from the herd and close in. A large deer or moose may try to defend itself with its hooves or antlers, or it may run into a river to escape. But, if they can, the wolves will corner and trap their prey, then pounce. They bite and pull at the animal's neck or tail end, dragging it down.

As they hunt, wolves stay downwind of their prey as much as possible. This means the wind is blowing toward them, and their scent does not blow toward the prey. That way, they get more of a chance to sneak up on it without being noticed.

HABITAT IN DANGER

The Ethiopian wolf, a rare wolf species, eats mainly mice and rats. But these prey animals are disappearing as wild land is replaced with crops, removing their natural habitat and food plants. As a result, the wolves have no food and also become endangered.

Two Eurasian wolves try to get good bites on a chamois, a type of mountain antelope.

Time to eat

Like many **predators**, when wolves have food, they eat as much as possible, in case it is a few days until their next kill. They can last for a week or more without eating, if they need to.

DID YOU KNOW?

The breeding male and female lead the hunt and pounce on the prey first—and they also get to eat first.

When eating an animal, wolves start with the main body organs, such as the heart and liver. They contain important vitamins and other substances that wolves need. Next, they eat the muscles (the part we normally think of as meat). Finally, if they are still hungry, they will munch on skin and bone.

Strong teeth and jaws let wolves chew tough meat, skin, and bone.

Eating tools

Wolves have big, strong teeth and powerful jaws for tearing and crunching flesh and bones. Their stomachs can stretch to hold up to 22 pounds (10 kilograms) of meat at once (the same as 100 hamburgers!). A wolf's stomach also contains a very strong acid. It breaks down bones and skin and kills germs.

If there is any meat left, wolves sometimes hide or bury it until they can come back to finish it off. If the pack has new cubs too small to go hunting, the wolves will also take meat back to the den for the cubs and their mother.

This wolf is carrying a small sheep, perhaps to use as food for the cubs in its pack.

HUMAN INTERACTION

In the past, when they were more common, wolves attacked humans quite often and sometimes killed and ate them. Today, though, it is very rare.

Are Wolves Endangered?

Wolves used to be the most widespread mammal in the world, apart from humans. Today, many countries that used to have wolves now have none at all.

Is the wolf safe?

The gray wolf, as a whole species, is actually not endangered. It is unlikely to become **extinct** (die out). That is because there are huge, wild areas of the world, such as northern Canada and Russia, where there are plenty of wolves and lots of wilderness for them to live in.

However, some subspecies (particular types) of gray wolf are in danger of dying out or are already extinct. Other species, such as the Ethiopian wolf, are endangered. You can see some examples below:

Name	Status
Mexican wolf (*Canis lupus baileyi*)	Endangered
Arabian wolf (*Canis lupus arabs*)	Endangered
Vancouver Island wolf (*Canis lupus crassodon*)	Endangered
Iranian wolf (*Canis lupus pallipes*)	Endangered
Red wolf (*Canis lupus rufus*)	Critically endangered (very endangered)
Bernard's wolf (*Canis lupus bernardi*)	Extinct
Texas wolf (*Canis lupus monstrabilis*)	Extinct
Newfoundland wolf (*Canis lupus beothucus*)	Extinct
Ethiopian wolf (*Canis simensis*)	Endangered
Maned wolf (*Chrysocyon brachyurus*)	Near threatened (may become endangered soon)

A maned wolf is an unusual type of wolf from South America. It is listed as "near threatened."

Threats to wolves

Unfortunately for wolves, there are many threats to them—especially if they live close to humans. Here are some of them:

- *Habitat loss*: Wolves lose their territories when land is taken over by humans.
- *Hunting by farmers*: Farmers poison, shoot, or trap wolves, in order to protect their own farm animals.
- *Hunting for sport*: People track and shoot wolves as a sport.
- *Food shortages*: Wolves run out of food because their prey species are endangered or hunted by humans.
- *Trapping for fur*: In the past, a lot of wolves were killed for their fur, and a few still are.
- *Disease*: Diseases can be caught from domestic dogs.

A grey wolf skin hangs on a wooden fence.

Wolfskin

In the past, many hunters made a living by trapping wolves for their skins. Wolfskin makes warm clothing and blankets. Arctic or tundra wolves had the most valuable skins. They live in cold, snowy regions, so have extra thick, soft fur. Wolfskin can be very smelly, but several thousand skins are still traded each year.

The Mexican wolf is a seriously endangered subspecies of gray wolf. In the past, many Mexican wolves were hunted to stop them from killing farm animals and deer.

HABITAT IN DANGER

The Tibetan wolf, a type of gray wolf, lives in and around the mountainous Himalayan region. Because of **climate change**, farmers there are moving farther and farther up the mountainsides to grow crops and herd their animals. This is reducing the Tibetan wolf's wild habitat, and it is now endangered.

Bring back the wolf!

Captive breeding involves breeding an endangered species in a zoo or wildlife **reserve**. Wolves are encouraged to mate, have cubs, and live as naturally as possible. If there are enough of them, and a good place to put them, they can then be **reintroduced** to the wild.

These **conservation** workers are releasing a red wolf into a forest in North Carolina.

HUMAN INTERACTION

Humans are mainly responsible for wolves disappearing and becoming endangered. But we can also work to help them. Besides reintroducing rare wolves, we can protect existing wild wolf packs. One way is to set up reserves, where wild land is protected and no one is allowed to build on it or use it for farms. There are also laws to ban wolf hunting in some countries.

The red wolf

The red wolf was hunted to extinction in the wild, but it survived in zoos and wildlife reserves. In the 1970s, experts in the United States began a captive breeding program to build up the numbers of red wolves in captivity. In 1987, they began to release them into wild forests. Despite some problems, the program has been a success.

Wolves in Scotland?

Thousands of gray wolves lived in Scotland until the 1700s. Some experts think reintroducing them to the country is a good idea, because it would help to control the huge numbers of red deer there. Others think it could cause problems for farmers and scare tourists.

These gray wolves are enjoying a wild lifestyle in Scotland, but they actually live inside a safe enclosure in a wildlife reserve.

What Other Animals Live in Packs?

Wolves are part of a larger family of wild dogs, the canids. They are all furry, meat-eating hunters, and they all have a similar "dog-like" appearance. A few canid species, such as the maned wolf, live and hunt alone or in pairs. But most live in packs.

Coyotes live in North America and Central America. They look similar to wolves but are smaller. Coyotes live in packs led by a breeding pair. Male cubs leave the pack when they are a few months old, but females stay for longer. However, coyotes mainly eat small prey, such as mice and lizards, so they do not need to go hunting in a pack. They usually hunt in pairs or alone.

Foxes are a type of small wild dog, and they are found all over the world. They live in small family groups. Usually, the female stays with the pups while the male goes hunting.

Dholes are small, reddish-brown wild dogs that live in Asia. They live in large packs of 10 or more animals. Sometimes several packs join together to make an even bigger group. Dholes, like wolves, work together to track and catch prey. They can kill animals that are much bigger than themselves, such as cows.

HUMAN INTERACTION

Unlike wolves, coyotes are good at surviving alongside people. Some live in towns and cities, where they raid garbage cans or steal pet food. Sometimes people even feed them.

You can tell a dhole by its reddish-orange coat, slender neck and head, and large, rounded ears.

The painted dog

The painted hunting dog, or African wild dog, gets its name from its blotchy, multi-colored coat. It forms the biggest groups of any wild dog. In the past, packs of up to 100 dogs roamed Africa. Now the species is rarer, and there are usually 10 to 20 dogs in a pack. The pack does everything together, even sleeping cuddled up in a pile. They all guard, feed, and care for the cubs as well as any pack member who is elderly, sick, or hurt.

A painted dog pack has two groups within it. The breeding female leads the female dogs, while the breeding male leads the males. These groups can sometimes split up and join up with other groups to make new packs.

This painted hunting dog pack lives in the Madikwe wildlife reserve in South Africa.

DID YOU KNOW?

Painted dogs make "chirping" noises like birds, to stay in contact when they are hunting together.

Painted hunting dogs are friendly and caring to each other—but not to their prey! They are fierce hunters, working as a pack to catch larger African animals such as antelopes, gazelles, and zebras.

Painted hunting dog pups are allowed to eat before the other pack members, and the whole pack will help to feed and protect them.

HABITAT IN DANGER

Painted hunting dogs are now endangered. As humans take over wild land for farming, the dogs lose their habitat and end up sharing space with farm animals. Farmers then kill the dogs to keep their own animals safe. The painted hunting dogs also die when they catch germs from pet dogs.

What's the Future for Wolves?

What will happen to wolves? They could become more and more rare, until they only live in the most faraway wildernesses and we rarely come across them. Or they could make a big comeback and become part of nature again in places where they have not been seen for centuries.

Some wild wolves have enough space to mark their territories, hunt together, and spread out to find mates. Arctic and Great Plains wolves should not die out. But it is a different story for some other species and rare gray wolf subspecies such as the Tibetan wolf. They will only survive with our help.

There are some parts of the world where the amazing sight of a wild wolf may become a thing of the past.

Can we live with wolves?

One of the most important ways to help wolves is to help people to understand them. Wolves are not that big, bad, dangerous, or scary—at least, not if they are left alone. We can live alongside them if we make sure that there is some space for the wolves and some for our farms and towns.

Governments can help farmers by paying them for animals eaten by wolves or by helping them find safe ways to keep wolves off their land.

Do you like wolves, or are you scared of them? Maybe it is a bit of both. What if scientists planned to reintroduce wolves near where you live? Would you be happy about it or worried?

Fact File

GRAY WOLF SUBSPECIES

This chart lists some of the many gray wolf subspecies and where they live.

Name	Description	Lives in...	Conservation status
White tundra wolf *Canis lupus albus*	Large, pale wolf with shaggy fur	Northern Europe and Russia	Least concern
Arctic wolf *Canis lupus arctos*	Large with thick white or cream fur	Northern Canada and Greenland	Least concern
Arabian wolf *Canis lupus arabs*	Very small wolf with pale brown fur and big ears	Saudi Arabia and nearby countries	Critically endangered
Mexican wolf *Canis lupus baileyi*	Small with reddish-brown fur	Mexico and parts of the southern United States	Endangered
Great Plains wolf *Canis lupus nubilus*	Medium-sized with gray or brown fur	Parts of Canada and the United States	Least concern
Common or Eurasian wolf *Canis lupus lupus*	Medium-sized wolf with dark gray fur	Forests in Europe and Russia	Least concern
Eastern timber wolf *Canis lupus lycaon*	Large white, gray, brown, or black wolf	The eastern United States and Canada	Least concern
Mackenzie Valley wolf *Canis lupus occidentalis*	Very big wolf with fur ranging from white to black	Western parts of Canada and the United States	Least concern
Iranian wolf *Canis lupus pallipes*	Small and skinny with light brown fur	Iran, Arabia, and surrounding areas	Endangered
Tibetan wolf *Canis lupus chanco*	Smallish wolf with beige or gray fur	Central Asia, China, and Korea	Endangered
Vancouver Island wolf *Canis lupus crassodon*	Medium-sized, gray or white wolf	Vancouver Island, Western Canada	Endangered
Red wolf *Canis lupus rufus*	Medium-sized with reddish fur and a pointed face	The eastern United States	Critically endangered

GRAY WOLF FACTS AT A GLANCE

Latin name: *Canis lupus*
Length: 3–6 feet (1–2 meters) long, including the tail
Height at shoulder: 24–35 inches (60–90 centimeters)
Weight: 33–154 pounds (15–70 kilograms)
Weight at birth: About 18 ounces (500 grams)
Lifespan: Usually around 10 years, but can be up to 18 years
Number of cubs in a litter: 2–12, but usually about 6 or 7
Number of wolves in a pack: Usually 4–12
Area of territory: Typically around 77 square miles
(200 square kilometers), but it can be as much as 1,160 square
miles (3,000 square kilometers)
Top speed: 37 miles (60 kilometers) per hour

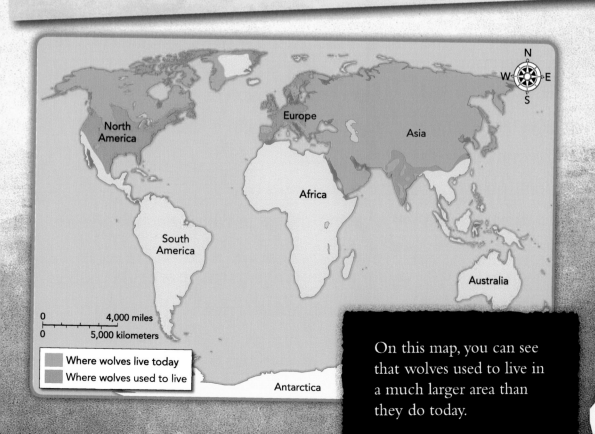

North America

Europe

Asia

Africa

South America

Australia

Antarctica

0   4,000 miles
0   5,000 kilometers

Where wolves live today
Where wolves used to live

On this map, you can see
that wolves used to live in
a much larger area than
they do today.

Glossary

adapt change to suit the surroundings

alpha name for the leading male or female in a pack

breeding pair leading male and female in a pack, which mate and have cubs

captive breeding breeding wild animals in zoos or wildlife reserves

captivity being kept in an enclosed zoo or park, instead of running wild

carrion rotting flesh from an animal that has already died

climate change changes in weather patterns, such as higher temperatures and more rain, that are happening partly because of human activities

conservation protecting wild living things or places and trying to save them from harm or damage

den shelter or hiding place used by wolves

ecosystem living and nonliving things in a particular area

endangered at risk of dying out

extinct no longer existing; has died out

food chain sequence of living things in which each feeds on the one before

food web number of linked food chains in a particular habitat

gland small organ that releases substances such as scent from the body

habitat natural home or surroundings of a living thing

litter set of young all born at the same time to the same parents

mammal hairy animal that feeds its young with milk from the mother's body

mate partner that an animal has babies with

predator animal that hunts and eats other animals

prey animal that is hunted and eaten by another animal

regurgitate bring food back up from the stomach

reintroduce release a species into the wild in a place where it once lived but has disappeared from

reserve protected area for wildlife to live in

species particular type of living thing

subdominant less important than the leader

subspecies different types of living thing within the same species

territory area of land that an animal marks out and guards as its own

track pick up on an animal's trail and follow it

wilderness wild land that has not been taken over or changed by humans

Find Out More

Books

Howker, Janni. *Walk with a Wolf*. Cambridge, Mass.: Candlewick, 2008.

Meinking, Mary. *Wolf vs. Elk* (Predator vs. Prey). Chicago: Raintree, 2011.

Simon, Seymour. *Wolves*. New York: Collins, 2009.

Zabludoff, Marc. *Dire Wolf* (Prehistoric Beasts). Tarrytown, N.Y.: Marshall Cavendish Benchmark, 2010.

Web sites

www.biokids.umich.edu/critters/Canidae/pictures/
This web site offers an amazing collection of photos of wolves and wild dogs, as well as recordings of sounds and other information.

kids.nationalgeographic.com/kids/animals/creaturefeature/ graywolf/
This is a good site to start with, as it provides basic facts, videos, maps, and cards to print out about gray wolves.

www.pbs.org/wgbh/nova/wolves/howl.html
This PBS web site tells about wolf howls, with real wolf howl recordings to listen to.

DVDs

The Language of Wolves (Canadian Geographic, 2002)
Wolves: A Legend Returns to Yellowstone (Warner, 2007)

Places to visit

International Wolf Center
1396 Highway 169
Ely, Minnesota 55731-8129
www.wolf.org/wolves/index.asp
Visitors can see real gray wolves here, and there is also lots of information presented about wolves.

Jacksonville Zoo and Gardens
370 Zoo Parkway
Jacksonville, Florida 32218
www.jacksonvillezoo.org
This zoo features a Florida wetland habitat where endangered red wolves roam.

More topics to research

Which parts of this book did you find the most interesting? What subjects would you like to know more about?

- Would you like to see real wolves? Many zoos around the world have gray wolves, other wolf species, or wild dogs that you can visit and view. Some, such as the International Wolf Center (see above), also have webcams, so you can watch their wolves on the Internet, wherever you are.

- Seeing real wolves in the wild is not so easy, but there are places where you can go on a wolf-spotting safari tour. They include Yellowstone National Park and parts of Alaska. If you do not live near any wild wolves, maybe you could go on a wolf-watching vacation!

- You, your family, or maybe your class at school could adopt a wolf in a reserve or a captive breeding program. You pay some money that goes toward caring for the wolf. The organization will then send you information on your adopted wolf and updates about its progress. Zoos, wildlife organizations, and wolf conservation groups often have wolf adoption information on their web sites.

Index